Troubleshooting Tips
for
Your Aga

D1637678

Troubleshooting Tips
for
Your Aga

Amy Willcock

EBURY
PRESS

1 3 5 7 9 10 8 6 4 2

First published in 2007 by Ebury Press, an imprint of Ebury Publishing

A Random House Group Company

Text © Amy Willcock 2007

Amy Willcock has identified her right to be identified as the author of this work under the Copyright, Designs and Patents Act 1988.

The Random House Group Limited Reg. No. 954009

Addresses for companies within the Random House Group can be found at www.randomhouse.co.uk

A CIP catalogue record for this book is available from the British Library

The Random House Group Limited makes every effort to ensure that the papers used in our books are made from trees that have been legally sourced from well-managed and credibly certified forests. Our paper procurement policy can be found on www.randomhouse.co.uk

Typeset by Palimpsest Book Production Limited, Grangemouth, Stirlingshire

Printed in the UK by CPI Mackays, Chatham ME5 8TD

Editor: Gillian Haslam
Illustrator: Melvyn Evans

ISBN: 9780091920159

CONTENTS

INTRODUCTION

Hi everyone

This book has come about as a result of the questions that arise in my Aga workshops and demonstrations. I have tried to cover most topics so that cooking with your Aga is delicious and easy, and I really hope you'll find the answers to any food and cooking queries on these pages.

I love to hear from readers so do drop me an email at amy@amywillcock.co.uk.

Amy

Buying an Aga

Which size Aga cooker should I buy?

If you have enough space in your kitchen, always choose a 4-oven Aga. However, 2-oven Aga cookers are the most popular and there is now the option of a 3-oven Aga which is the same size as the 2-oven. See page 21 for more details.

Do I need another cooker?

No – if you are cooking the Aga way and using the 80/20 rule (see page 29) you will be fine (but a separate hob is useful).

What about buying a second-hand Aga?

There are lots of companies selling second-hand and re-conditioned Aga cookers. Most Aga distributors sell second-hand Aga cookers obtained from clients upgrading their Aga cooker so it is worth enquiring about these. There are a few important questions you should ask before parting with your cash:

- How old is the Aga, how many previous owners has it had and does it contain asbestos products?
- Does it have a guarantee?
- Does the Aga have the appropriate mandatory approval?
- Will it be fully installed by an Aga-trained engineer and are they CORGI-registered (a legal requirement)? Aga cookers are designed to be built on site so do not accept one that has been moved fully assembled.

Buying an Aga

- What installation charges are included in the price? Assembly charges? Delivery charges? Does the company deliver directly to the kitchen?
- Will the company service the Aga?
- Has the cooker been converted from one fuel to another? (See page 13 for more info.)
- Have any parts been replaced? If so, have they been replaced with genuine Aga parts? If not, have the parts just been cleaned up and painted?
- Has it been re-finished? Is it painted or vitreous enamelled?
- Is there a charge for a colour change?
- Is cookware supplied with the Aga?

Age is a major consideration. An Aga cooker may be 40 years old and working perfectly well in its original environment. However, when moved or converted to suit a new home, it may not work as well as it should and the cost can be almost as much as a new one.

What about buying a converted Aga cooker?

Do be wary of converted Aga cookers. A converted Aga is usually one that has been converted from solid fuel to oil, or occasionally converted to gas. As every Aga is hand-built to specific fuel requirements, it is always a risk to buy a converted Aga for two reasons – safety and performance.

The safety of the cooker could be affected by the altering or modifying of the product and will nullify the approval and, in the case of gas-fired products, could be illegal. The performance of the Aga could certainly be affected as the original performance is difficult to achieve if modifications have been made.

How much does it cost to run an Aga?

Depending on the type of Aga cooker you have (be it a 2-, 3- or 4-oven Aga) oven and which energy company you buy your fuel from, the price will vary and it is now difficult to put even an approximate price tag on what it costs to run an Aga without knowing all the details. However, the price can be worked out using the technical pages on the Aga website. Look under fuel consumption at www.aga-rayburn.co.uk

How environmentally-friendly is an Aga cooker?

The jury is still out on this topic because the new biofuel-ready Aga has only just come on to the market.

If you take into account that Agas are made from recycled materials and that most Aga cookers last a life time, then that is at least halfway to the tackling the environmental issues. The Aga factory itself has invested heavily to ensure that the emissions from the foundry are 'as clean as the air you breathe'.

Aga-Rayburn is also encouraging customers and helping them to consider the possibility of generating their own energy from wind, solar, water or even earth energy to power their Agas. Look at the Aga website www.aga-rayburn.co.uk for further information or to book a visit from an engineer.

What sort of cooking equipment should I buy?

See page 46 for my recommended list of equipment.

How the Aga Works

Why does Aga-cooked food taste so good?

The reason foods taste so much better when cooked in an Aga is because they retain valuable moisture, which is usually lost during conventional cooking. This is because in some cases the surface of the food is sealed by the Aga cooker's unique radiant heat. The air in a conventional oven is generally hotter than in an Aga; the hotter the air, the more moisture it will absorb, which can dry food out.

How does an Aga work?

It doesn't matter whether your Aga is powered by gas, electricity or oil as a burner heats them all in the same way. The heat from the burner unit is transferred to the ovens and hot plates where it is stored. When the insulated lids are down, they hold in the heat. When the lids are up, heat is lost.

All the ovens on the right-hand side of the Aga are externally vented, keeping cooking smells out of the kitchen and succulence in the food. The stored heat is released as radiant heat, which is what locks in the flavour and moisture, giving such superb results. Heat lost through cooking is automatically restored.

How can I tell what the oven temperatures are?

The Aga is thermostatically controlled, so you don't need to worry about exact temperatures. New Aga users might find it useful to hand an oven thermometer in the middle of the ovens first thing in the morning to see what the temperatures are. Do this only once, just to give you an indication of the heat level.

What's the purpose of the heat indicator?

The heat indicator should be checked first thing in the morning to confirm that the Aga is up to heat. The mercury should sit on the black line, which means that the Aga has its full amount of stored heat. Although I have come across Aga cookers where the mercury is in the black and they are fully up to heat, this is a rare occurrence. If this happens to a newly installed Aga, ask your Aga dealer to check it out. This is where the quirks of the Aga can be so different. It is quite usual for the mercury to drop during cooking but don't worry as the heat will automatically be restored.

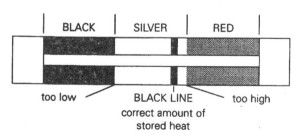

I only turn off my Aga for its annual service, and once the temperature has been reset I don't touch it until the next service. After installation or servicing, make a note of the mercury position for the first few mornings, and move the control up or down until the mercury consistently reaches the black central line.

How do I know when to use the ovens and when to use the plates?

There is one fundamental rule in Aga cooking – *keep the lids down and cook in the ovens*. About 80 per cent of all cooking should be done in the ovens and only 20 per cent on the plates. The Aga cooker's combustion system, heat path and insulation schemes are designed on this basis. If you follow this rule, you will never suffer heat loss again. If you need more heat, before you move the control knob, consider whether you should be using the ovens more.

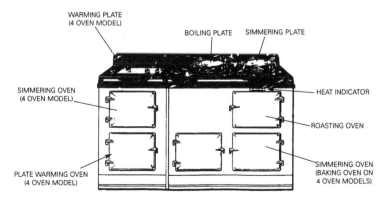

What are the different plates for?

The Boiling Plate

The Boiling Plate is situated directly over the burner, making it the hottest plate. It is used when you want a fierce or high heat to bring foods to the boil or for stir-frying. Bread is toasted on it using the Aga Toaster. It is also where a kettle is brought up to the boil.

The Simmering Plate

The Simmering Plate gives off a gentle heat ideal for simmering, but the biggest advantage is that you can cook directly on it, like you would with a griddle. Season it as you would a new frying pan by putting a little vegetable oil on a piece of kitchen paper and wiping the plate's surface. Do this two or three times, leaving the lid up so that some of the oil burns off and does not leave an oily build-up. If you don't use the plate as a griddle for a while, re-season before use.

To cook on the plate, lift the lid a few minutes before cooking to reduce the heat a little, wipe the surface with a small amount of oil and proceed with cooking. Remember, too much oil makes smoke! I cook pancakes, fried eggs, toasted sandwiches and tortillas like this. I always use the square pre-cut piece of Bake-O-Glide (see page 50) on the Simmering Plate. This eliminates the need for seasoning the plate and requires little, if any, oil, giving a low-fat cooking option.

Always close the lids promptly on both plates when you have finished using them, otherwise precious heat escapes. Each plate takes three large saucepans.

The Warming Plate (4-oven Aga only)

The Warming Plate is to the left of the Boiling Plate and is a very useful area for warming awkwardly shaped serving dishes and teapots. It is also great for resting large joints of roasted meat.

What are the different ovens?

The 2-oven Aga has a Roasting Oven and a Simmering Oven. The 4-oven Aga has a Roasting Oven, a Baking Oven, a Simmering Oven and a Warming Oven. The 3-oven Aga is basically the same as a 2-oven Aga with the addition of a Baking Oven.

As there are no dials to control the temperatures, food is cooked by position and timing. If you think in those terms, adapting conventional recipes will become second nature. Looking at food while it is cooking is not a problem because the cast-iron ovens retain the heat all around the inside of the oven and opening the door will not result in sudden heat loss.

Recipes sometimes specify cooking dishes on particular runners. The runners in the ovens are counted from the top downwards.

New Aga-oven users sometimes find they burn their arms when using the ovens. Avoid this by using the oven reach (see page 47) to retrieve pans from the back of the ovens and wearing gauntlets.

What should I cook in the Roasting Oven?

The Roasting Oven is the hottest oven, providing four different areas of cooking space:

High: top of the oven
Middle: centre of the oven
Low: near the bottom
Floor: the oven floor

The oven is slightly hotter on the left side, which is near the burner.

High: the top of the oven is perfect for cooking foods that require a very high heat, such as grilled bacon and Yorkshire puddings, or for crisping the tops of cottage pies or browning meat.

Middle: this is place for cooking joints of meat. Timings for roasts cooked here are the same as for conventional cookers. However, some roasts can be started here and then finished off in the Simmering Oven, but timings will be longer. For 2-oven Aga owners, this is the area to use for baking but you will need an item of cookware called an Aga Cake Baker (see page 97). It is essential for cakes that need more than 40 minutes' baking time. The cake baker is really an 'oven within an oven', creating a moderate temperature for a longer amount of time.

For cakes requiring less than 40 minutes, using the Cold Plain Shelf in the Roasting Oven creates a moderate oven temperature, but only for about 20–30 minutes. Once the plain shelf absorbs the oven's heat, it is useless until it is taken out and cooled. The Plain Shelf must not be stored in the Aga – it must go into the Aga cold. Four-oven Agas do not require a Cake Baker as they have a Baking Oven. Crumbles, muffins and cookies also cook well here.

Low: cook roast potatoes, bread and sponge cakes here. When making sponge cakes, do not use the Cake Baker; instead use heavy-based tins and place the grid shelf on the floor of the Roasting Oven and the plain shelf on the second set of runners just above, to reduce the heat and create a moderate oven temperature.

Floor: I use this part of the oven the most. Think of the Roasting Oven floor as an extension of the hot plates – anything you can cook on the hot plates you can do on the Roasting Oven floor. Use it to fry foods such as onions or eggs or for browning meats. Heat a frying pan with a little oil in it on the floor of the Roasting Oven; add your ingredients and fry.

Do not put wooden or Bakelite-handled pans into the Roasting Oven. A useful piece of cookware to buy is the Aga Grill Pan. By heating it up in the Roasting Oven you can 'grill' foods in it. Bread can be baked directly on the floor with fantastic results, also pastry tarts and pies.

What should be cooked in the Baking Oven?

This oven is only available with the 3- or 4-oven Aga cookers. It is perfect for all types of baking as it is a moderate oven. It can also be used like the Roasting Oven but with longer cooking times. The top of the oven is slightly hotter.

Top of the oven: ideal for baking small cakes.

Centre: for baking brownies, muffins, biscuits, breads and crumbles. It is also the correct temperature for baking fish.

Bottom: when cooking soufflés or cheesecakes here, they must be off the floor. Slide a grid shelf onto the oven floor and stand the tin or dish on the grid shelf.

What do I use the Simmering Oven for?

This is the slow oven. On the 2-oven Aga it situated bottom right; on the 4-oven Aga it is found top left. On the 2-oven Aga it has three sets of runners; on the 4-oven model there is only one set in the middle.

The gentle heat of the Simmering Oven is ideal for slow cooking and cooking overnight. Everything to be cooked in this oven, apart from meringues and a few other recipes, must be started either on the hot plates or in the Roasting Oven and brought up to the boil before going into the Simmering Oven. It is fine to put wooden and Bakelite-handled pans in the Simmering Oven, and use saucepans with tightly fitting lids that can be stacked on top of each other.

Centre: this is where casseroles, soups and stocks are made. Bring to the boil on the Boiling Plate, then transfer to the Simmering Oven. Roasts such as lamb and pork can be started in the Roasting Oven, then moved to the Simmering Oven, leaving space in the Roasting Oven for other dishes. Rice puddings and baked custards are also started in the Roasting Oven, then transferred to the Simmering Oven for slow, gentle cooking. The temperature is also perfect for steamed puddings.

Bottom: if you don't have a Baking Oven, this is where fruitcakes and meringues are cooked. Pinhead oatmeal can be brought to the boil on the Boiling Plate, then placed on a grid shelf on the floor of the oven and left overnight for creamy porridge the next morning. This is the best place for drying fruits and vegetables, such as tomatoes and mushrooms, or infusing oils.

Floor: the floor of the Simmering Oven is ideal for cooking rice and root vegetables. The Aga method for cooking for rice (see page 121) produces delicious fluffy rice, while the Aga way with root vegetables (see page 79) is extremely easy and nutritious.

How do I use the Warming Oven?

Available only in the 4-oven Aga, this is primarily a place to keep things warm. It is where plates and serving dishes are warmed, and wet shoes stuffed with newspapers are dried out. It can be used to dry out fruits and vegetables like the Simmering Oven but they will take much longer.

How to Cook with your Aga

When cooking Sunday lunch, I run out of heat when cooking the roast potatoes or Yorkshire pudding. How can I prevent heat loss?

This question crops up at every workshop or demonstration I do. The answer is simply to examine your method of cooking. When people ask me this, I throw the question back at them and ask how many rounds of toast they've cooked and how many kettles have been boiled using the plates rather than the ovens.

Heat loss often occurs if you use the hot plates too much beforehand. Perhaps you cooked breakfast on top rather than in the ovens that morning? Or par-boiled potatoes on the Boiling Plate instead of in the Simmering Oven. Check how much the lids are up. **Remember to stick to the golden rule of 80 per cent of cooking to be done in the ovens and 20 per cent on the plates.**

If you still have problems after double-checking you are doing everything correctly, you are probably not planning your cooking timetable correctly for the menu you have chosen. For instance, Yorkshire pudding can be cooked first thing in the morning when the ovens are at their hottest and successfully re-heated just before serving. Roast potatoes can be cooked up to their final 20 minutes the day before and then blasted in the Roasting Oven. And even green vegetables can be blanched the day before, ready to be re-heated just before serving. Good cooking, whether you are using an Aga or conventional cooker, is all about planning and preparation.

You often talk about planning your cooking space – what does this mean?

To get the best use out of your Aga ovens, you need to plan how to use the space. This is something that will become second nature after you've been coking with an Aga for a while.

An easy way to do this is to use the plain shelf. Put the cold shelf on your work surface and arrange the pieces of cookware you need to use on top of it or put the empty cookware you plan to use inside the oven. Take into account grid shelves and, if you can, stack pots and pans. Aga pots and pans are made with flat lids for this reason, but if you are using conventional saucepans with ovenproof handles, invert the lids if possible and carry on stacking (but check that the lids will be safe and not fall in). When stacking pans, always point the handles in the same direction and use tins that fit directly onto the runners for maximum oven capacity.

As you fill the Warming or Simmering Ovens, try to put the foods you are serving first at the front.

Try to plan your menu around your Aga. Consider logistics. Invariably food moves around the Aga during the cooking process, usually ending up in the Warming or Simmering Ovens, on the Warming Plate or on protected hot plate lids. Plan to use the space they leave in the ovens well. You may find that you cook food in a different order compared to conventional cooking as the safety net of the Simmering or Warming Ovens allows for greater flexibility.

Decide which recipes can be cooked ahead and take into account thawing times and re-heating times if applicable. Serve some foods that can be completely prepared and cooked ahead and just need re-heating.

Look at your dishes cooking and baking in the Aga frequently and don't be afraid to move the food around to another location in or on your Aga. If a hot plate is too hot, then move it. The recipe timings in my books are guidelines as every Aga is different. The Aga creates intuitive cooks because of this. You will learn to cook by instinct.

How do I know whether to use the hot plates or the ovens?

As a general rule, if a dish needs more than 7 minutes of cooking time, use one of the Aga ovens, not the hot plates.

Which cooking methods are best suited to which Aga plates or ovens?

Boiling: use the Boiling Plate. Once boil is established, move to the Roasting Oven floor.

Braising: bring up to the boil on the Boiling Plate for 5–10 minutes, then transfer to the Simmering or Baking Oven.

Browning meat: use the first set of runners in the Roasting Oven, then move to the Roasting Oven floor.

Frying: use the Roasting Oven floor.

Grilling: use the Aga grill pan on the Roasting Oven floor or on the Boiling Plate.

Poaching: bring to the boil on the Boiling Plate, then move to the Roasting or Simmering Oven depending on food being poached (poach eggs on the Simmering Plate).

Roasting: Roasting, Baking and Simmering Ovens – use the Roasting Oven for conventional timings and the Baking and/or Simmering Ovens for slow roasting.

Simmering: start on the Boiling Plate, cover with a lid, then move to the Simmering Oven. To reduce liquids, remove the lid and continue in the Simmering Oven.

Steaming: start on the Boiling Plate or in the Roasting Oven, cover, and then move to the Simmering Oven.

Stir-frying: pre-heat the pan or wok in the Roasting Oven, then use the Boiling Plate.

Toasting: always pre-heat the Aga toaster to prevent bread sticking to it, then place the bread in the rack and toast on the Boiling Plate. Close the lid, but keep an eye on it as it will toast very quickly; turn over to toast the other side. If you prefer crispy toast, leave the lid open.

My problem is that I forget that I have dishes cooking in the Aga. Do you have any tips for remembering when cooking times are up?

Tie a bright red ribbon around the rail or above the Aga so that it catches your eye and reminds you something is in the oven. A magnet with a note attached works well too.

Timers are also crucial to the Aga cook so make sure you place them where you'll hear the alarm ring. Alternatively, buy a timer on a long cord so that you can wear it around your neck – this means you will hear the timer wherever you are. I prefer digital timers as they are the most accurate.

I have several favourite recipes written for conventional cooking. How can I convert them for Aga use?

Converting conventional recipes for Aga use is easy. As all Aga cooking is done by timing and position, just remember how the heat is distributed in each oven and once you decide where the food is to be cooked, adjust the timings accordingly. I tend to underestimate the time by roughly 10 minutes, as I can always put the dish back in for a little longer if necessary.

Take a standard muffin recipe as an example. The ingredients and method are exactly the same. The recipe calls for a pre-heated oven, a temperature of 180°C/350°F/gas mark 4 and a cooking time of 40–45 minutes. Make up the muffin mixture according to the recipe and pour into the muffin tin.

For the 2-oven Aga:

There is no need to pre-heat the oven as the Aga is always ready to cook. I would use the lower/bottom half of the Roasting Oven, but not the Roasting Oven floor. Place the grid shelf on the floor of the Roasting Oven and the cold plain shelf (to make a moderate oven temperature of 180°C/350°F/gas mark 4) on the second set of runners. Estimate the cooking time at 30 minutes, but they may take up to 45 minutes if the oven is not right up to temperature. Check after about 25 minutes. The muffins are done when pale gold on top and shrinking away from the sides of the tin.

For the 3- and 4-oven Aga:

Prepare as above but cook in the Baking Oven, omitting the cold plain shelf until it is needed (probably 20–25 minutes into the cooking time).

What are the average temperatures of the Aga ovens?

These are the typical centre-oven temperatures:

Warming Oven

Warm – approximately 70–100°C/150–200°F/gas $\frac{1}{4}$

Simmering Oven

Slow – approximately 135–150°C/260–300°F/gas 1–2

Baking Oven

Moderate – approximately 180–200°C/350–400°F/gas 4–6

Roasting Oven

Hot – approximately 240–260°C/475–500°F/gas 8–9

Caring for
your Aga

How can I keep my Aga in that pristine, straight-out-of-the-showroom condition?

There is a very simple solution to being the proud owner of a clean Aga – avoid getting it dirty in the first place! If you use the ovens for cooking foods that splatter (such as during frying and grilling), the hot plates will stay clean. Pushing pans to the rear of the ovens will keep the aluminium door clean as well. Keep a damp cloth ready to wipe up spills as they happen. Acidic liquids and milk can cause pitting to the enamel top. Don't drag pans across the top or the surface will eventually scratch.

What's the best way to clean the ovens?

One of the greatest bonuses of cooking in an Aga is that the chore of oven cleaning doesn't really exist. The ovens self-clean because the constant high heat means that food spills carbonise and only need to be brushed out with the wire brush or, if your vacuum cleaner has a metal nozzle, use it to suck out the carbonised bits at the bottom of the oven.

The Aga doors must NEVER be immersed in water as this would destroy the insulation. To clean the doors, simply lay out a double thickness of tea towels on a flat surface and then carefully lift off the doors from their hinges. Wear gauntlets when moving the doors as they will be very hot. Lay the doors enamel side down on the tea towels and leave to cool for a few minutes. Using a damp wire wool scouring pad and a little washing-up liquid, firmly go over the inside of the door – this will scratch the aluminium but it won't harm it. Wipe clean and replace the doors on the hinges.

To clean the outside of the oven doors and the enamelled front and top, use a proprietary mild cream cleaner. Lightly apply it with a damp cloth, then wipe with a dry cloth to polish off any residue. A silicone polish can also be used on the front and top of the cooker to help control the dust. This is a good idea for darker-coloured cookers, where the dust tends to be more visible.

How do I clean the hot plates?

Firstly, protect open lids from splatters by draping a tea towel over the back (remove before closing the lid) or use the Bake-O-Glide Simmering Plate Splatter Protector.

Use the wire brush to clean the hot plate surfaces. Food will burn off so you only need to clear away any carbonised bits that will interfere with the contact between saucepan bottoms and the hot surface. It's useful to keep the wire brush handy when making toast so that you can clear away breadcrumbs instantly.

To clean the inside of the Simmering Plate lid, lift the lid and leave open for a few minutes to cool slightly, then place a grid shelf over the hot plate and the plain shelf on top of the grid shelf. This will reduce the heat, allowing easier cleaning in the middle of the lid. The grid shelf also acts as a safety barrier in case your hand slips. Use a soapy wire wool pad and a damp cloth. The inside of the lid will scratch but it will not affect the cooker's performance. The Boiling Plate lid rarely needs cleaning as the intense heat keeps it clean.

Clean the chromium lids with a soapy damp cloth and buff with a clean dry tea towel. Do not use wire wool or any harsh abrasives on the chrome. To avoid the tops of the lids being scratched, either use the specially designed round Aga oven pads or protect with a folded tea towel if you place dishes on top. Don't put heavy pans or tins on them as this may cause dents.

If grease collects around the very edge of the plates, gently scrape it away with the blade of a craft knife, but take care not to scratch the enamel.

If you have guests staying with you, try to make them 'Aga Aware' before they use the cooker so that scratches, spills and dents are avoided.

What happens if I spill water into the hot plate?

Any spillage will be absorbed into the insulation material. The one thing that is likely to cause a problem is spilt milk because of the odour emitted when drying out so it would be wise to remove the contaminated rockwool and replace it with fresh material.

When should I have the Aga serviced?

Always use an authorised Aga distributor to service your Aga. If you move into a house with an Aga, try to find out its service history from the previous owners, plus the contact details for the company that has serviced it in the past. Gas and electric Aga cookers should be serviced once a year and oil-fuelled Aga cookers every six months. The standard check and service will take about an hour.

The night before a service, remember to turn off your Aga so that it cools down. Turn the burner off and leave the pilot on (refer to the inside of the burner compartment door). After servicing, the Aga technician will re-light the Aga.

What happens to the Aga if I have a power cut?

As the heat in an electric Aga is stored up like a storage heater, the cooking facility would be maintained for one day but as the fan would not be operating the heat in the oven would be considerably reduced, progressively getting worse with the duration of the power failure. Gas Aga cookers carry on indefinitely, but the power to the fan will turn off immediately. The oil-fired Aga cooker will remain alight, however it will operate on a reduced heat until the power is reinstated.

Aga Cooking Equipment

Do I need to buy new saucepans and casserole dishes to use on my Aga?

One of the first things all new Aga owners want to know is whether they have to buy new saucepans. The easy answer is no, because most people will have some suitable cookware already. However, if you use pans that are not suitable, you will waste valuable heat time and energy and there will be a marked difference in cooking times. Cast iron, earthenware, ceramic and copper are all suitable for the Aga. Glass Pyrex can also be used in the ovens on the grid shelves.

To test if your existing saucepans are suitable for the Aga, fill each one with cold water and put it on the Boiling Plate. Hold each side of the pan down and see if it rocks. If the pan is flat, tiny bubbles appear uniformly over the bottom of the surface – this means it is suitable for Aga use. It is not flat if the bubbles appear only in certain areas of the pan.

Saucepans with wooden or Bakelite handles are not suitable for use in the Roasting Oven. Buy pans that are fully ovenproof and that can be used anywhere on the Aga. Saucepans and casseroles should be as wide as possible so that they cover most of the hot plate surface. The flat lids on many pans enable stacking in the ovens, giving masses of room for cooking.

I've just started to cook on an Aga. What basic Aga cooking kit do I need?

The basic Aga kit comprises:

2 grid shelves
Large roasting tin and grill rack
Half-size roasting tin and grill rack
1 plain shelf
1 toaster
1 wire brush

I do recommend buying a couple of extra half-size roasting tins, and 2-oven Aga owners will find another plain shelf useful if a lot of baking is to be done.

I also suggest that you gradually build up a collection of the following items. Don't be alarmed by the length of this list – many pans can be collected over the years and do not need to be purchased all at once. I have marked the items I consider essential with an asterisk.

1 x 9 litre stainless steel stockpot *
2 x 1.5 litre stainless steel shallow casserole dish *
2 x 2.7 litre stainless steel sauté casserole dish *
2 x 1.25 litre stainless steel shallow saucepan *
1 x non-stick milk pan *

1 x cake baker * (only required by 2-oven Aga)

2 x half-size hard anodised shallow baking tray (fits directly onto the runners) *

2 x full-size hard anodised baking tray (fits directly onto the runners, can also be used as a plain shelf)

2 x half-size hard anodised tray bake

1 x full-size hard anodised tray bake

1 x cast iron grill pan *

1 x 1.5 litre hard anodised kettle *

1 x 3.5 litre aluminium interior non-stick coated kettle

1 x cast iron sauté pan

2 x 18cm loose-bottomed hard anodised sponge tins *

2 x 20cm loose-bottomed hard anodised sponge tins *

1 x hard anodised universal pan and lid *

1 x hard anodised deep roasting tin

1 x oven reach (useful for getting tarts out of the oven) *

What are the best baking tins for Aga use?

When buying tins for the Aga, make sure that they slide onto the runners. This means the full capacity of the ovens will be used. The one tin that I use constantly is the half-size shallow hard anodised baking tray. The full-size one can also be used as a plain shelf. They are sufficiently heavy duty to use on the hot plates and are ideal for things like roasting potatoes.

Make sure muffin and other specialised tins are also as heavy duty as possible. Cake tins must be heavy duty. As dark colours absorb heat more quickly than lighter, you may find in some cases a darker cake tin will require a slightly shorter cooking time than, say, a lighter aluminium cake tin.

Any advice on buying a kettle to use on the Aga?

To get the best from your kettle, buy a size that suits your needs. There is no point having the 3-litre kettle if your household only has two people in it. I have a 'baby' kettle for everyday use. Bring out the great kettle only for large gatherings such as Christmas.

A common complaint about kettles is that they become pitted at the bottom and can take a long time to come to the boil. The first problem occurs when boiled water is not fully used and the water level is just topped up. This is bad practice as the boiled water leaves mineral deposits sitting on the base of the kettle which cause pitting. When this happens, it takes longer to bring water up to the boil and the kettle is less efficient. Using a smaller kettle ensures you use all the water when making pots of tea so the kettle is always filled with fresh water. If you are using a large kettle, only fill it with the amount of water needed for the job. If you live in a hard-water area, it is essential to descale the kettle once a week.

I have had a cold water tap fitted by my Aga. If you are having an Aga installed in your kitchen, it's well worth considering this as it makes filling kettles and saucepans so easy.

You often recommend using Bake-O-Glide. What is it?

Bake-O-Glide is an amazing non-stick, re-useable paper used to line tins, making cleaning so easy, or used directly on the Simmering Plate. It is dishwasher-safe and only small amounts of fat are needed, if at all, to make surfaces non-stick. Roast potatoes crisp up beautifully and the crunchy bits left in the tin lift off easily. It is available in rolls and in pre-cut sizes. I use the pre-cut piece on the Simmering Plate to fry eggs, cook pancakes and make toasted sandwiches. See page 125 for stockists.

Meat and Poultry

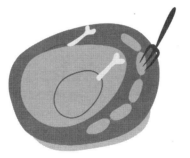

Why is meat roasted in an Aga so good?

Roasting a joint of meat in the Aga is easy and the radiant heat locks in the flavour, making it a truly different eating experience altogether. For meats like lamb and pork, you can use the slow-roasting method (see below) or cook it conventionally. For good cuts of meat, veal and beef, I suggest using the fast roasting method (see below).

Slow-roasting method:

Prepare the joint for cooking. Cut a couple of onions in half and put them into a tin lined with Bake-O-Glide. Sit the joint on top of the onions and slide the tin onto the fourth set of runners in the Roasting Oven for 30–40 minutes or until it begins to brown, then transfer to the Simmering Oven for approximately double the amount of conventional cooking time. Weigh the joint before cooking to calculate the timings.

Conventional fast-roasting method:

Prepare joint as above and calculate the roasting time according to the cut and type of meat. When it is finished cooking, rest for 15–20 minutes before carving.

Meat and Poultry

What are the average Aga cooking times for different meats?

Beef

Rare: 12 minutes per 450g

Medium: 15 minutes per 450g

Well done: 20 minutes per 450g

Lamb

Pink in the middle: 15 minutes per 450g

Well done: 20 minutes per 450g

Pork

25 minutes per 450g

Veal

15 minutes per 450g

What is the best Aga method for cooking fillet of beef?

This method of cooking a whole fillet of beef results in a beautifully rare middle. For a 900g fillet, add about 2 tablespoons of dripping to the large roasting tin and place on the Roasting Oven floor. When the fat is smoking, transfer the tin to the Boiling Plate and seal the meat on all sides. The fat will splatter so keep a damp cloth handy to wipe up any mess. Remove the excess fat, then hang the tin on the third set of runners in the Roasting Oven. Cook for no more than 15–20 minutes.

When the cooking time is up, take the fillet out of the oven and remove from the tin. Do not wash the tin. Wrap the meat very tightly in cling film, twisting the ends for a snug fit. Put the fillet onto a plate and leave it to rest for at least 20 minutes on top of the protected Simmering Plate. To serve the meat, remove the cling film, put the meat back into the tin and put the tin on the Roasting Oven floor for 8–10 minutes, just to heat it through. Serve straight away.

How do I roast a chicken in the Aga?

This is my method is for roasting chicken and all poultry.

Line the roasting tin with Bake-O-Glide. Cut an onion in half (use two for a large chicken) and place the chicken on top of the onion. Stuff the cavity of the chicken with herbs, onion or lemon and season with salt and pepper. Rub over butter or oil or lay strips of bacon over the chicken; rub in more salt and pepper. Slide the tin onto the lowest set of runners in the Roasting Oven and set the timer. Check halfway through cooking and cover the chicken with foil if it is browning too quickly.

Approximate timings for roasting a whole chicken:

900g chicken (small): 35–45 minutes
1.5kg chicken (medium): 45–60 minutes
2kg chicken (large): $1^1/_2$–$1^3/_4$ hours
3kg chicken (very large): 2 hours

To test if the chicken is cooked, pierce the thigh with a skewer; if the juices run clear, it is cooked. If they are pink or red, the chicken is not ready so cook for a little longer. Rest the chicken for 15 minutes before carving.

What is the best Aga method for roasting duck?

Put the duck into a colander and pour over a kettle full of boiling water – this helps to loosen the fat. Drain the duck and dry it really well inside and out with kitchen paper. Brush the duck with a little brandy (alcohol helps to dry out the skin, giving a crispier finish).

Hang the duck up by its wings with a plate underneath in a place where it won't be eaten by the cat and where there is a cool breeze (the air helps to keep the duck really dry). Alternatively, place uncovered in the fridge. This can be done a day in advance, but it must be left hanging for a minimum of 6 hours.

To cook the duck, put it onto a grill rack in a roasting tin and hang it on the third or fourth set of runners in the Roasting Oven. Cook for 1–2 hours, depending how big the duck is. I like the meat practically falling away from the bones and really crispy skin, but if you want your duck rarer, only cook it for roughly an hour.

When the duck has finished cooking, remove it from the oven and allow it to rest for 5–10 minutes.

How do I roast a pheasant in the Aga?

Line the roasting tin with Bake-O-Glide. Place the bird(s) in the tin, rub generously with butter or lard (or even cover with the paper that the butter was wrapped in) and season with salt and pepper. If you wish, cover the breasts with bacon. Stuff the cavity of the pheasant with half an onion or apple and season with salt and pepper. Slide the tin onto the third set of runners of the Roasting Oven and set the timer for 45–50 minutes. Baste halfway through cooking.

To test if the pheasant is cooked, pierce the thigh with a skewer; if the juices run clear, it is cooked. Be careful not to overcook game – as the fat content is lower, it does have a tendency to dry out.

How do I roast other game birds?

Cook as for pheasant (see above) but adjust the cooking times.

Partridge: Roast for 15–18 minutes.

Grouse: Roast for 20–30 minutes.

Woodcock, snipe and quail: Roast for 12–15 minutes.

How do I roast a turkey in the Aga?

The Aga can accommodate a turkey weighing up to 12.5kg and I recommend using a deep roasting tin. There are two methods of roasting turkey: the slow-roasting method, which can be done overnight, and the conventional method. The advantage of the slow method is that you don't have to worry about the turkey and the Roasting Oven will be available for cooking all the traditional trimmings. Timings are approximate and very much depend of the size of the bird. The timings may have to be increased for older Agas if you use the slow-roasting method.

The conventional method of cooking the turkey will use up a lot of heat so planning and preparation are very important.

Preparing a fresh turkey

Wash the turkey with water and pat dry with kitchen towel. Stuff only the neck end of the bird. Put a couple of onions into the body cavity and season well with salt and pepper. Put the turkey into the roasting tin. Do not truss the bird. Generously brush melted clarified butter all over the bird and season with salt. The secret of a succulent golden bird is in the basting. Leave the pot of clarified butter at the back of the Aga so that it is within easy reach for basting about every 30 minutes if cooking the bird conventionally.

Slow-roasting method

Place the roasting tin directly on the floor of the Roasting Oven and cook for about 1 hour or until the turkey is browned. A larger turkey may take longer to brown. It is essential to give the turkey a blast of heat for a good amount of time for food safety. When it is browned, baste with the clarified butter, cover loosely with foil and move to the Simmering Oven for the following times:

3.6–4.5kg: 3–6 hours
5–7.25kg: 5–8$\frac{1}{2}$ hours
7.25–9kg: 8$\frac{1}{2}$–11 hours
9–11kg: 11–13$\frac{1}{2}$ hours
11–12.8kg: 13$\frac{1}{2}$–15$\frac{1}{2}$ hours

All times are approximate.

Conventional or fast-roasting method

Place the roasting tin on the Roasting Oven floor or hang on the last runner if it will fit. After about 1 hour, or when the turkey is browned, cover loosely with foil and cook for the following times:

3.6–4.5kg: 1$\frac{3}{4}$–2 hours
5–7.25kg: 2–2$\frac{1}{2}$ hours
7.25–9kg: 2$\frac{1}{2}$–3 hours
9–11kg: 3$\frac{1}{2}$–4$\frac{1}{2}$ hours
11–12.8kg 4$\frac{1}{2}$–5$\frac{1}{2}$ hours

All times are approximate.

The turkey is done when the thigh juices run clear when pierced with a skewer. Rest the turkey for at least 20 minutes. A large bird will stay hot for a long time and can withstand a long resting time so take this into consideration when working out your cooking timetable.

When using the conventional roasting method, you can start cooking the turkey breast side down, turning it breast side up about 45 minutes before the end of the cooking time. This way of cooking ensures the breast meat will be even more succulent.

How do I cook goose?

This method is based on a 2.5-3kg goose with giblets and gizzard – you may need to adjust the cooking times for different weights.

Put a grill rack into a roasting tin. Put the goose onto the grill rack, prick the skin with a fork and rub salt all over the bird really well. Slide the tin into the Roasting Oven and cook for 1 hour, then move down to the Simmering Oven and continue cooking for a further 1–2 hours or until the goose is cooked and the skin is crispy. What you want to end up with is the meat practically falling away from the bones and really crispy skin. Pour off and reserve all the goose fat – it's brilliant for roasting potatoes in.

Meat and Poultry

What's the best cooking method for chops?

Heat the Aga grill pan on the floor of the Roasting Oven until it smokes. Transfer the grill pan to the Boiling Plate. Add the chops and place the pan back on the Roasting Oven floor for 4–5 minutes, depending how thick the chops are. Turn the chops over and cook for a further 4–5 minutes until cooked through.

How do I cook spare ribs in the Aga?

Ribs taste better if they have been marinated for an hour or more before cooking. Drain the ribs from the marinade. Line a roasting tin with Bake-O-Glide and lay the ribs on top. Hang the tin from the fourth set of runners in the Roasting Oven and cook for 40 minutes. Pour your sauce over them and transfer to the Simmering Oven for 1–2 hours or until the meat is tender.

How should sausages be cooked?

Lay the sausages on the grill rack in the roasting tin. Slide the tin onto the top runners in the Roasting Oven. Cook for 20–30 minutes, turning halfway through cooking so they brown on all sides.

How do I cook rack of lamb?

Cook the rack of lamb in the Roasting Oven for only about 15 minutes – it does depend on the size of the rack but the worst thing to do is to overcook it.

What's the best way to cook bacon on an Aga?

For crispy bacon, cook the rashers on Bake-O-Glide in a shallow baking tray on the Roasting Oven floor.

How do I cook a steak in an Aga?

Place a grill pan on the Roasting Oven floor and let it heat up so that it is very hot – I sometimes leave mine in all day if I know I will be cooking steak later on. When you are ready to cook the steak, move the grill pan to the Boiling Plate and cook to your liking. It is vital to have a grill pan to cook steak on an Aga.

What's the Aga method for making stock?

Roast off the meat bones in the Roasting Oven for about 45 minutes or until brown, then put them into a large pot and cover with cold water. Add herbs, seasoning, half an onion, a chopped up carrot, celery, garlic and anything else you fancy (but not starch-based vegetables such as potatoes). Bring to the boil on the Boiling Plate and boil rapidly for 5–10 minutes. Cover with a lid and transfer to the Simmering Oven for at least 6 hours or overnight. Skim off fat and strain through a sieve. Store in the fridge for up to a week, bringing to the boil before using, or freeze for up to 3 months.

To make chicken or game stock, use a whole carcass, but do not brown. Start it in cold water.

Basic casserole

You can change the meat in this basic recipe to suit the season. The method for making a casserole is exactly the same and the Aga really comes into its own with this type of recipe.

Serves 6

65g flour
1.7kg meat (e.g. chuck steak, chicken pieces, pork), cut into 4cm cubes
100ml cooking olive oil
150g pancetta cubes or chopped bacon
8 shallots, peeled and quartered
2 garlic cloves, peeled and crushed
450ml wine, to suit meat – red for beef, white for chicken or pork
600ml good stock, to suit the meat
zest of 1/2 lemon (optional, but good with chicken)
salt and pepper

herbs, to suit the meat:
pork: lemon thyme, flat leaf parsley, bay leaf
beef: thyme, flat leaf parsley, bay leaf
chicken: tarragon or rosemary or sage (not all three) and flat leaf parsley

1 Put the flour into a plastic bag and shake the meat pieces in it. You may have to do this in batches.

2 Heat half the oil in a large casserole dish and brown the meat pieces in batches (don't overcrowd the pan). You can do this on the Roasting Oven floor or on the Boiling Plate. Put the browned meat to one side.

3 Heat the rest of the oil in the same casserole and add the pancetta or bacon and cook for a few minutes, then add the shallots and cook for 5 minutes or until they are soft. Add the garlic, but be careful not to let it burn.

4 Pour the meat and the juices back into the casserole and add the wine, stock and herbs (and zest, if using) and season with salt and pepper. Bring to the boil on the Boiling Plate, then cover and transfer to the Roasting Oven for 20–30 minutes.

5 Remove from the Roasting Oven and stir. Move to the Simmering Oven and cook for a further 2½ hours.

How do I make gravy on the Aga?

It doesn't matter what sort of meat you are roasting as the method is the same. I use onions as a rack for the meat to sit on while it is roasting. You can vary the fruit jelly to suit the meat the gravy is to accompany, such as apple jelly for pork or mint jelly for lamb. You can use less stock for thicker gravy, or more for a thinner consistency. The quality of the stock is paramount – if you use inferior stock you will end up with inferior gravy. Always use home-made stock (see page 63).

Cut two onions in half and rest the joint on top. When the joint is cooked, remove it from the tin, cover with foil and let it rest for 15–20 minutes. Spoon off any excess fat from the tin, leaving about 1–2 tablespoons with the meat juices and onions.

While the meat is resting, put the tin directly into the Simmering Oven and bring the juices to a simmer. Add 1 tablespoon of flour to the fat, onions and meat juices and whisk it in. Keep whisking until the flour absorbs all of the fat, adding a little more flour if necessary. Whisking constantly so that there are no lumps, pour in about 100ml wine (optional). Add a tablespoon of redcurrant jelly. Still whisking, pour in about 500ml stock.

Bring the gravy to a rapid simmer and cook for about 5 minutes. Add salt and pepper to taste. It is important to cook out the flour (and wine, if using). Strain the gravy into a warmed jug and keep hot at the back of the Aga or in the Simmering or Warming Oven.

Fish and Seafood

Why is Aga-cooked fish so good?

The Aga is perfect for cooking fish as it locks in the juices at the same time as crisping up the skin. One of the most amazing things about the Aga is that fish can easily be cooked in the same oven as, for example, a fruit tart or sponge cake without the transference of smell or taste.

How do I poach fish?

For a whole fish, such as a salmon, use the conventional fish kettle method. Make a court bouillon by filling a fish kettle with water, herbs, peppercorns and lemon halves, then put in the whole fish. Bring to the boil on the Boiling Plate (if the fish kettle is large, use the Simmering Plate as well). As soon as it has boiled for 5 minutes, remove the kettle from the heat and leave the fish to cool in the liquid. This method cooks fish really well and you can forget about it while it cools down.

How do I fry fish in the Aga?

Pour some sunflower oil into a heavy-based shallow pan to a depth of 2–3cm. Place the pan on the floor of the Roasting Oven and heat until smoking. Batter the fish or coat in breadcrumbs. Remove the pan from the oven, add the fish to the pan and return to the Roasting Oven floor. Fry for a few minutes on each side in the pan or until the batter or breadcrumbs are golden.

Fish and Seafood

Can the Aga be used for steaming fish?

Steaming fish in the Aga is easy. Lay a large piece of foil on a shallow tin and butter the inside of the foil. Lay the fish on the buttered foil and season with herbs, lemons, salt and pepper. Spoon over 1 tablespoon of white wine or water, and then wrap up the foil into a loose parcel, fully sealed but with enough room for steam at the top. Slide the tin onto the third set of runners of the Roasting Oven and cook for 10–12 minutes or until the fish is cooked to your liking. Owners of 4-oven Agas can also use the Baking Oven, although the fish will take a little longer to cook.

What's the best way to cook kippers?

Place the kippers in a roasting tin. Add about a tablespoon of water to the bottom of the tin and place a knob of butter on top of each kipper. Cover with foil and cook in the Roasting Oven for 8–10 minutes. If they are on the bone, they may take longer.

My children love fish fingers. How do I cook them in the Aga?

Place the frozen fish fingers on a baking tray on the Roasting Oven floor, then move to third set of runners (total cooking time about 10–12 minutes). Also, see page 83 for Aga oven chips.

How should I cook shellfish?

It is best to cook shellfish for as little time as possible. Things like mussels, clams, etc only need to be steamed open so cook on either the Boiling or Simmering Plate.

I roast lobster in the Roasting Oven, but you do have to brave and not squeamish as you must drive a knife through their heads first. Of course, you can boil them in a pan on the Boiling Plate as well.

Scallops are superb simply sealed in a smoking pan that has been heated in the Roasting Oven first, then moved to either the Boiling or Simmering Plate. You can also use a piece of Bake-O-Glide on the Simmering Plate and cook the scallops directly on that.

A grill pan is also really useful for cooking squid, scallops and almost any other fish – heat it up so that it is really hot in the Roasting Oven and then move to the Boiling or Simmering Plate and add the fish.

What's your recipe for fish stock?

Follow my basic meat stock recipe on page 63, but do not brown the fish bones, and only cook for about an hour. Fish stock can be kept in the fridge for up to 3 days.

Fish and Seafood

Lemon and lime fish cakes

My basic recipe for fish cakes uses cod, but you can adapt it for different types of fish.

Serves 4

500g mashed potatoes (no added butter – see step 1)
500g cod fillet, cut into large chunks
2cm red chilli, deseeded and finely chopped
2cm fresh ginger, grated
1 tbsp fish sauce
1 tbsp chopped fresh coriander
zest of 1 organic lemon
zest and juice of 1 organic lime
1 egg
salt and pepper
sunflower oil, for frying

1 To make mashed potatoes, bring the potatoes up to the boil in a pan of water on the Boiling Plate and boil for 3–4 minutes. Drain off all the water, cover with a tightly-fitting lid and transfer to the Simmering Oven for 20–30 minutes or until the potatoes are soft. Mash in the usual way, but without adding butter or milk.

2 Simply throw all the ingredients except the sunflower oil into a food processor and process until everything is combined but not smooth. Using wet hands, pull off tablespoons of the mix and shape into patties. (At this stage you can chill the fish cakes in the fridge and fry later if you wish. Remove the fish cakes from the fridge at least 20 minutes before cooking.)

3 Heat about 2 tablespoons of oil in a large shallow baking tray lined with Bake-O-Glide on the floor of the Roasting Oven. When it is hot, 'fry' the fish cakes – put the fish cakes on the tray and cook in the Roasting Oven for 15 minutes, then turn over and continue cooking for another 15 minutes or until they are crispy on the outside.

Fish pie

Serves 6

250g undyed smoked haddock, chopped into small pieces
650g cod, cut into small pieces
8 scallops, sliced in half horizontally
16 tiger prawns, shelled and vein removed
4 hard-boiled eggs, peeled and cut into wedges
2 heaped tbsp freshly chopped flat leaf parsley, plus extra
to garnish
zest and juice of 1 lemon
salt and pepper
30g butter
30g flour
450ml hot milk
30ml double cream

Mashed potato topping:

900g potatoes, peeled and cut into chunks
generous knob of butter
120ml sour cream or crème fraîche
salt and pepper
30g Gruyère cheese, grated

1 First, make the mashed potato topping. Put the potatoes into a saucepan of salted water and boil on the Boiling Plate for 3 minutes, then drain the water and transfer to the Simmering Oven for 20–25 minutes. Drain well. Put them through a potato ricer until creamy and fluffy. Beat in the butter and sour cream and season. Set aside.

2 Butter a large, deep, ovenproof dish. Put all the fish and seafood into the dish and add the egg, parsley and lemon zest. Season.

3 To make the sauce, melt the butter in a pan on the Simmering Plate and add the flour, stirring all the time. When all the flour has been absorbed into the butter, slowly add the milk little by little, stirring constantly. When all the milk has been used, add the lemon juice. You should have a smooth white sauce. Pour in the cream and season. Simmer the sauce for 3–4 minutes so that it is slightly thicker and glossy.

4 Pour the sauce over the fish. Mix well so that everything is coated with the sauce.

5 Spread the mashed potato over the fish, then sprinkle over the cheese. The pie can be made to this point 24 hours in advance. Remove the pie from the fridge 20 minutes before cooking to bring to room temperature.

6 Cook the pie on the third set of runners in the Roasting Oven for 35–45 minutes. The top of the pie should be crispy, bubbling and enticingly browned.

Fish and Seafood

Vegetables

What's the best Aga way to cook root vegetables?

Root vegetables can be cooked very successfully in the Aga, retaining most of their valuable vitamins as well as their taste.

Prepare the vegetables in the usual way. Peel or scrub them and put into a saucepan of salted water. Bring the saucepan to the boil on the Boiling Plate and cook with the lid on for 4–5 minutes. Remove the pan from the heat and drain off all the water. Replace the lid and put the pan on the Simmering Oven floor. Potatoes will take approximately 25–30 minutes to cook but the timing really does depend on the size of the vegetables being cooked. I usually cook carrots for about 15 minutes as I like them with a bit of a bite.

The amazing thing about this method of cooking vegetables is that if for some reason the meal is delayed, the vegetables happily sit in the Simmering Oven for up to 3 hours without burning. It is true to say they would be well done, but they would still be edible, neither falling apart nor burnt.

If you have ovenproof serving tureens with tight-fitting lids, you can use them like a saucepan. Once the veg have boiled for 4–5 minutes, drain, tip them into the tureen and cover. They will cook in the tureen in the Simmering Oven.

Vegetables

You often refer to 'get-ahead green veg'. What does this mean?

Restaurants often use this method of cooking vegetables. Have ready a large bowl of water with some ice in it. Put it to one side. Cook your green vegetables for 2–3 minutes in rapidly boiling water so they are tender. Using a slotted spoon, transfer them from the boiling water straight into the bowl of iced water (this is what is meant when a recipe says 'blanch'). The iced water stops the vegetables cooking further and helps them retain their colour. Drain well on kitchen paper and put into an ovenproof dish. Brush over a little melted butter or olive oil and cover with foil. Leave in a cool place or the fridge for up to 24 hours.

To serve, season with salt and pepper and put the dish (still covered with foil) on the floor of the Roasting Oven for 15–20 minutes. Open the door and when you hear the fat spitting, they should be ready. Serve immediately. You can easily do all your vegetables this way and group them together in an ovenproof serving dish.

What about cooking green veg conventionally?

Cook green vegetables, such as French beans, peas, mange tout, etc, in the conventional way. Bring a pan of water to the boil and cook them in salted boiling water for as long you like, then drain and serve.

What are 'get-ahead roast potatoes'?

This is a great way to cook roast potatoes in advance. Peel the potatoes and parboil in a pan of water on the Boiling Plate for 8 minutes, then drain and fluff up by putting the lid on the pan and shaking. Put the dripping or other fat into the half- or full-size roasting tin and place on the floor of the Roasting Oven to heat up. When the fat is smoking, add the potatoes, baste with the fat and cook on the Roasting Oven floor for 25 minutes. Take them out of the oven, turn them over and let them cool. Cover them with foil and put aside until ready to finish off. They can be prepared up to this point 24 hours ahead of time. Do not refrigerate.

To serve, remove the foil and put the potatoes back in the Roasting Oven for 25 minutes. Serve straight away. Timings may have to be adjusted to suit the size of the vegetables. This method can also be used for parsnips.

How about roasting potatoes in the traditional manner?

Line the large roasting tin with Bake-O-Glide and put about 2 heaped tablespoons of dripping or goose fat into it. Place on the Roasting Oven floor until it is really hot and smoking. Bring the potatoes up to the boil in a saucepan of water on the Boiling Plate and cook for 5–8 minutes or until they start to soften around the edges. Drain off all the water and, with a lid on the saucepan, shake it so that the potatoes are roughed up on the outer edges. Remove

Vegetables

the tin from the oven and place on the Simmering Plate. Add the potatoes to the hot fat, baste and move them back to the floor of the Roasting Oven. Cook for about 50 minutes or until crisp.

How do I cook new potatoes using the Aga?

Place the potatoes in a large pan of salted water. Bring to the boil on the Boiling Plate for 3 minutes. Drain off all the water, cover the pan with a lid and transfer to the Simmering Oven. Cook for about 30 minutes or until tender.

Which oven do I use for baked potatoes?

Wash the potatoes and place on a grid shelf on the third set of runners in the Roasting Oven for 45–60 minutes (the cooking time depends on the size of the potatoes).

What is the best way to make mashed potato on the Aga?

Put the potatoes into a saucepan of water and bring to the boil on the Boiling Plate. Boil for 3 minutes. Take the pan off the heat and drain off all the water. Replace the lid and transfer to the Simmering Oven for 20–30 minutes. When the potatoes are tender, break them up with a knife or a potato ricer. Mash in butter and crème fraîche. Season with lots of salt and black pepper. If the potatoes are too stiff, add either some more crème fraîche or a little milk.

My children love oven chips – how can I make my own?

Peel the potatoes and cut into thick strips. Soak them in cold water for 10 minutes, then drain very well on a tea towel – the drier the potatoes are, the better the chips will be. Put the potatoes into a large bowl and pour in some sunflower oil – about 1 tablespoon for every 2 potatoes. Toss the potato strips in the oil, ensuring they are evenly coated. Spread the potatoes on a large baking tray and cook them on the floor of the Roasting Oven for 35–45 minutes, turning occasionally, until they are brown and crisp on all sides. Remove from the oven and sprinkle generously with salt before serving.

How do I dry vegetables in the Aga?

Cut the fruit or vegetables into slices 1–2cm thick or into halves or quarters. Lay them on a shallow Aga baking tray lined with Bake-O-Glide. Slide the tray into the Warming Oven in a 4-oven Aga for 6–8 hours or overnight. The juicier the fruit, the longer it will take to dry out. In a 2-oven Aga, slide the tray onto the third set of runners in the Simmering Oven for 3–6 hours. Leave mushrooms whole and start them in the Simmering or Warming Oven, then transfer to the lid of the Boiling Plate, protected by a tea towel or an Aga circular chef's pad until they are really dry. Store in an airtight bag or jar and rehydrate with boiling water when you want to use. Some vegetables can also be stored in olive oil, either with or without herbs.

Vegetables

What about Aga dried tomatoes?

Remove any stalks from tomatoes, cut in half, remove seeds and lay them cut side up on a piece of Bake-O-Glide on a baking sheet. Drizzle over some olive oil, a little salt and pepper and a sprinkling of caster sugar if desired. Place them in the Simmering Oven for about 5–6 hours, but keep an eye on them as you don't want them to brown. When the tomatoes are firm and dry, take them out and leave to cool. Sterilise a jar and put the cooled tomatoes in with some basil, garlic, thyme or any other herb you choose, cover them with good-quality olive oil and seal. Keep them in the fridge.

Fruit and Preserving

What are your tips for Aga jam-making?

There are a few golden rules when making jams, jellies and marmalades. Make them when your Aga is at its hottest, such as first thing in the morning. Always use dry, unblemished fruit. All equipment must be scrupulously clean and glass jars and lids must be sterilized. If you have a dishwasher, put them through a high heat cycle, then place on a baking tray and put in the Simmering Oven for 10–15 minutes. Keep them warm when you pour in the jam. Seal the jars while still hot.

Warm sugar and fruits in the Simmering or Warming Oven before using. If a recipe uses fruit that needs to be cooked before adding sugar, do it in the Simmering Oven. Use as little water as possible and cover the fruit with a tightly fitting lid. Bring to the boil on the Boiling Plate, then transfer to the Simmering Oven until ready.

Skim the scum off frequently when the jam is boiling or add a small knob of butter to disperse it.

To test for a good set, put a few saucers into a freezer before you start to cook the jam. After the first 20 minutes or so of rapid boiling, take a saucer out of the freezer and drop a small spoonful of the jam onto the cold saucer. Allow it to cool for a minute, and then push your finger through the jam. If it wrinkles, it is ready; if not, boil the jam for a few minutes more. Carry on testing until a set has been reached. Always remove the jam from the heat when testing so that if it is ready you will not overcook the jam.

Fruit and Preserving

Basic chutney

This is a basic recipe for chutney. You can adjust the fruit and veg to suit the season. Remember to stone fruits and peel veg with a tough skin, such as pumpkins and squashes. If you wish, pep up the chutney with a teaspoon of dried chilli flakes or a minced fresh chilli. The same rules apply to the preparation of jars and seals as in jam making (see page 87).

Makes about 6–8 jars

1kg vegetables such as courgettes
1kg acid fruit, such as tomatoes or plums
1kg apples or pears, peeled
500g onions, peeled
500g sultanas or raisins
500g brown sugar
700ml cider vinegar
150ml water
about 1 tsp sea salt

For the spice bag:
6 allspice berries
blade of mace
1 tsp black peppercorns
1 tsp coriander seeds
about 4cm fresh ginger, sliced

¹/₂ tsp cloves
and/or anything else you want to put into the bag

1 You will need a largish square of muslin and some butcher's string for the spice bag. Spread out the muslin, put all the spices into the middle, then gather up the corners and tie tightly with string.

2 All the vegetables should be deseeded and chopped, and tough peel removed. Tomatoes should be skinned and deseeded, but fruits like plums can just be stoned and chopped.

3 Put all the ingredients into a large heavy-bottomed stainless steel pan (do not use copper or aluminium for this) and heat slowly on the Simmering Plate until the sugar dissolves.

4 Move to the Boiling Plate and boil for 3–4 minutes, then transfer to the Simmering Oven for 2–3 hours or until very thick and a spoon leaves behind a clean trail. Ladle into sterilised jars and seal. Leave to age for a minimum of 1 month before using.

Fruit and Preserving

What's the trick for opening hard-to-turn jam-jar lids?

Opening stubborn new jar lids could not be simpler. Invert the jar top onto the Simmering Plate for a few seconds and you will hear it release. Protect your hands with a tea towel before touching the hot metal lid.

Strawberry jam

Makes 4 x 400g jars

1kg jam sugar
2kg strawberries
juice of 1 lemon

1 Put the sugar into a preserving pan or large heavy-bottomed saucepan (not cast iron), and place in the Simmering Oven to warm.

2 Hull and pick through the strawberries, discarding any blemished fruit. Put the fruit in the preserving pan, add the lemon juice and move the pan to the Simmering Plate. Stir constantly until all the sugar has dissolved and the fruit releases its juices.

3 Move to the Boiling Plate and boil rapidly for 4–5 minutes. Skim off any scum as it appears. Test for a set then, using a jam funnel, spoon into the sterilised jam jars. Seal tightly with a screw-top lid while it is boiling hot.

What's the best way to poach fruit on an Aga?

Place the prepared fruit in a saucepan. Add any flavourings such as sugar, honey, spices or a cinnamon stick, and just enough water to cover the fruit. Cover the pan with a lid, place on the Boiling Plate and bring to the boil. Transfer to the Simmering Oven for 2–3 hours or until the fruit is soft and plump.

Which oven should I use for baked apples?

Core the apples and score the peel horizontally around the middle of the fruit. Place in a roasting tin lined with Bake-O-Glide. Stuff the apples with some sultanas or other filling of your choice and top with generous knobs of butter. Slide the tin onto the third set of runners in the Roasting Oven and bake for 30–35 minutes or until the apples are tender but still hold their shape. If they brown too much, move to the fourth set of runners and place the Cold Plain Shelf on the second set of runners. For 4-oven Aga owners, bake in the Baking Oven for 40–45 minutes.

Fruit and Preserving

Cakes and Baking

Can you give me some general guidelines on baking in the Aga?

- Plan to do your baking when you know your Aga will be slightly cooler, such as after a large cooking session.

- Warm flour and sugar needed for recipes either at the back of the Aga or in the Simmering and Warming Ovens.

- Buy two Cold Plain Shelves – you can cool them down quickly by running them under cold water, but having an extra one will save this task.

- Use the black surface area of the top of the Aga to melt butter or chocolate for baking.

- Keep a kettle of boiling water going on the top of the Simmering Plate to lower an oven temperature.

- Refresh stale bread by spraying with water and baking it in the Roasting Oven for 5 minutes.

Why is the Cold Plain Shelf so important when baking?

Baking is where the Cold Plain Shelf comes into its own. So many Aga owners use it as an extra shelf, rendering it completely useless for the job it is intended for. I really do recommend buying a second Cold Plain Shelf if you are a keen baker. It must be kept outside the Aga, not inside one of the ovens. The Cold Plain Shelf will give you a moderate oven for about 30–40 minutes. So if you are a 2-oven Aga owner, for cakes requiring more than 40 minutes use a Cake Baker (see page 97). For 4-oven Aga owners, use the Baking Oven, although you will notice some recipes start off in the Roasting Oven.

Which part of the oven should I use when baking?

As a general rule, I have found that the best positions for baking cakes are either with the grid shelf on the lowest set of runners in the Roasting Oven with the Cold Plain Shelf above on the second set of runners, or with the grid shelf on the floor of the Roasting Oven and the Cold Plain Shelf on either the third or fourth set of runners, depending how high the cake tin is. Most cakes (apart from fruit cakes) take roughly 20 minutes to cook. Check the cake regularly while it is baking; opening the oven door will not impair the finished cake – in fact, I have cooked a Victoria Sponge with the oven door completely off and it was fine.

Do I need special tins and bakeware for Aga use?

Good-quality tins are crucial when baking, and the heavier they are, the better the results will be. I recommend all tins should be hard anodised items. You may find that darker coloured tins require a shorter cooking time than lighter ones (such as aluminium) because dark colours absorb head more quickly. Loose-bottomed or spring-form tins are so much easier to use.

Thin tins are unsuitable for Aga use because the heat passes through them too quickly, so the outside of the cake may burn before the centre is cooked.

The oven reach is essential for pulling out tarts, breads and pizzas from the Roasting Oven floor.

How do I use the Aga Cake Baker?

Using the Aga Cake Baker means there is no need to turn cakes during baking and no worry of them over-browning.

To use the Cake Baker, select the correct-sized tin and remove the trivet and cake tins from inside the cake baker. Put the outer container and lid onto the Roasting Oven floor to heat up. Pour the cake mixture into the tin and remove the Cake Baker from the oven. Set the trivet and cake tin inside the Cake Baker. Replace the lid and put it on the Roasting Oven floor. Set the timer.

How do I know what to bake where?

Here's my quick, at-a-glance guide:

Bread: Roasting Oven floor.

Cheesecake: grid shelf on the Roasting Oven floor with the Cold Plain Shelf above for 5–10 minutes, then move to the Simmering Oven for 35–45 minutes. You can start it in the Baking Oven for 15–20 minutes, and then move to the Simmering Oven.

Cookies and biscuits: fourth set of runners in the Roasting Oven or third set of runners in the Baking Oven.

Drop scones and tuiles: use the Simmering Plate covered with a round piece of Bake-O-Glide.

Frozen bread: fourth set of runners in the Roasting Oven; grid shelf on the floor of the Roasting Oven.

Frozen pastry cases: Roasting Oven floor.

Melting chocolate/butter: back of Aga on black enamel top, on the Warming Plate or in the Simmering Oven for 10 minutes.

Muffins: grid shelf on the floor of the Roasting Oven or fourth set of runners with the Cold Plain Shelf on the runners above; Baking Oven on third set of runners.

Pancakes: directly on the Simmering Plate surface using a piece of Bake-O-Glide or wipe a small amount of oil onto the surface.

Pizza: floor of the Roasting Oven for approximately 12 minutes.

Popovers: heat tin on the Roasting Oven floor, pour in batter, then move up to third set of runners.

Scones: third set of runners in the Roasting Oven.

Sponge cakes: grid shelf on the Roasting Oven floor with the Cold Plain Shelf on the third set of runners.

I have a 2-oven Aga but no Cake Baker. Can I still bake successfully?

A really good baking tip for 2-oven Aga owners is to use the Cold Plain Shelf as a hot shelf. If you have a recipe that requires a longer cooking time, over 40 minutes or so, and don't have a Cake Baker, you will need to move the cake from the Roasting Oven to the Simmering Oven. The best way to continue the baking is to slide the Cold Plain Shelf (even if you don't need it) into the Roasting Oven to heat up so when you need to move your cake to the Simmering Oven, you move the shelf as well. Slide the now 'hot' Plain Shelf onto the desired runner, and continue baking the cake on it. The hot plain shelf gives an extra boost of heat to the cake and oven.

My cake-making isn't always successful. Where could I be going wrong?

These are the most common baking problems I'm asked about:

Cracked top

The cake has usually been baked in too hot an oven or has been positioned too close to the top of the oven or the Plain Shelf. The top of the cake sets and therefore makes it very difficult for the gas to spread evenly around the cake.

Cake with a raised middle

This happens when a cake is put in an oven that's too hot, then moved to too low a temperature before the outside of the cake has a chance to set. It can also occur if the mixture hasn't been creamed enough.

Sunken centre

There are three reasons for this happening: too much raising agent, too hot an oven and a third reason which happily doesn't apply to Aga owners – slamming a conventional oven door soon after the cake has gone in lets in a sudden rush of cold air and changes the pressure in the oven, shaking the air out before the cake has a chance to set.

Burnt bottom

The most obvious reason for a burnt cake bottom is too thin a tin – see page 96 for guidance on the best tins to use for Aga baking. The other problem that can occur is not enough air circulating around the cake tin, as can be the case if you use the Plain Shelf instead of a grid rack. For fruit cakes and cakes requiring long baking times, start the cake off on the Grid Shelf then, when the cake is set, transfer it to a Hot Plain Shelf. To cool an oven and for extra absorption of heat in an oven, place a roasting tin containing either clean sand or water on the floor or the lower shelf.

Many conventional tart recipes recommend blind baking. Is this necessary with an Aga?

Pastry-lined tart tins do not need to be blind-baked when using an Aga. Line the tin with raw pastry, add the filling and place on the Roasting Oven floor with the cold plain shelf above. The pastry base will cook at the same time as the filling, so you won't end up with soggy pastry.

Cakes and Baking

All-in-one Victoria sponge cake

Serves 6–8

175g self raising flour
175g soft unsalted butter
175g caster sugar
1 tsp vanilla extract
3 large eggs
1 rounded tsp baking powder

1 Line two 20cm round sponge tins, preferably loose bottomed, with Bake-O-Glide. Put all the cake ingredients into the bowl of an electric mixer and, using the beater attachment, beat until combined. Divide the cake mix between the prepared cake tins.

2 Place the grid shelf on the floor of the Roasting Oven and place the cake tins towards the right side of the oven, on the grid shelf. Slide the Cold Plain Shelf onto the third set of runners and bake the cakes for 20 minutes or until they are golden on top, gently coming away from the sides and spring back when lightly pressed on top. For 4-oven Aga owners, cook the cakes on the fourth set of runners in the Baking Oven for 20–25 minutes and use the plain shelf only if the cakes are browning too quickly.

3 Remove the cakes and stand on a wire rack for a minute, then remove the cakes from the tins and cool on the wire rack.

What's the best way to bake a fruit cake in the Aga?

When it comes to baking your fruit cake, the best oven in the world is the 2-oven Aga Simmering Oven. Prepare your fruit cake recipe as usual, then place the tin on the third set of runners in the Simmering Oven. On average, a 20cm round fruit cake will take anything from 4 to 10 hours. The reasons for the huge timing variation are that no two Aga cookers are the same and the newer ones have better insulation. My standard fruit cake recipe in the Simmering Oven takes about 6 hours.

Owners of a 4-oven Aga may find their Simmering Oven is slower than a 2-oven Aga Simmering Oven. The cake will probably cook better if started in the Baking Oven for 45–60 minutes, then transferred to the Simmering Oven in as high a position as possible and cooked for 4–10 hours or even longer in some cases. Another trick is to use the large grill rack from the large roasting tin. Put the grill rack directly onto the Simmering Oven Floor and put the cake tin on it for cooking. If you feel you don't need the extra boost of the Baking Oven, bake the cake in the Simmering Oven only as above.

Lining the tin with Bake-O-Glide is all the tin preparation you need. There's no need for brown paper or newspaper for lining and covering the cake. Another good method for cooking fruit cake is the Aga Cake Baker (see page 97). The only drawback is that you are restricted to the size and shape of the tins.

Fruit cake

Makes a 23cm round cake or a 20cm square cake

575g currants
225g sultanas
225g raisins
60g organic glacé cherries, rinsed, dried and chopped
60g organic candied peel
zest of 1 organic orange and 1 organic lemon
1 tbsp treacle
4 tbsp brandy
275g soft unsalted butter
275g soft brown sugar
275g plain flour
60g rice flour
$\frac{1}{2}$ tsp salt
1 tsp mixed spice
5 eggs
60g chopped almonds

1 Read the advice on fruit cakes on page 103. The day before making the cake, put the dried fruit, peel, zests, treacle and brandy in a bowl and mix well. Cover with cling film and leave in a cool place to marinate.

2 Line your tin with Bake-O-Glide if necessary or if the tin is new.

3 When ready to make the cake, cream the butter and sugar together until pale and fluffy. Sieve the flours, salt and mixed spice together in a bowl. Add the eggs to the butter mix one at a time, alternating with the flour mix until it is all incorporated. If you are doing this with an electric mixer, use a very low, gentle speed. If you do it by hand, use a folding motion to mix.

4 Fold in the fruit with all the juices and the almonds. Spoon into the prepared tin.

5 Bake in the Roasting Oven for 20 minutes, then transfer to the Simmering Oven for 5–10 hours, depending on your Aga. You can bake it just in the Simmering Oven but it will take longer. The baking time will vary tremendously from Aga to Aga and will take as long as it takes! The great thing about an Aga is that you can open the door and keep on checking.

Any advice on baking bread in the Aga?

Prove yeast-based recipes and bread dough next to the Aga – it can cut the proving time in half in some cases.

I rarely use a loaf tin for bread. I make my bread into rustic shapes and bake directly on the Roasting Oven floor. Take a shallow baking tray and turn it over. Put a sheet of Bake-O-Glide on top of the upturned baking tray and transfer the shaped dough on top. Place the baking tray halfway into the oven, then carefully slide the tray out, leaving the Bake-O-Glide and bread in the oven.

How can I achieve a crisp bread crust in the Aga?

The Aga's Roasting Oven is just like a baker's oven. Buy a small cup-sized stainless steel beaker or mould. Fill it with cold water and place in the Roasting Oven when baking bread. This will create the steam which is essential in achieving a good crust. You can also splash water directly onto the Roasting Oven floor for an instant blast of steam. It's good to do this halfway through baking and just before the final 8 minutes of baking.

For a really crispy base crust, sprinkle the Bake-O-Glide with the polenta or finely sieved stale breadcrumbs and place the dough on top.

Refrigerator white bread

Makes 1 loaf

1kg strong white bread flour
600ml hand-hot water
25g butter, softened
30ml sunflower oil, plus more for greasing
25g salt
35g fresh yeast

1 Put the dough hook into an electric mixer and add the flour, butter, oil and salt. Mix to combine.

2 Crumble the yeast into 425ml of warm water, stir and when the yeast has melted, pour it into the flour. Add more warm water (to a maximum of 175ml) if the dough is too stiff. It is best to hold back a little water and add if necessary rather than pour it all in and have to add more flour.

3 Knead for 8 minutes on a medium speed or until the dough is soft and elastic. Lightly oil a bowl and put the dough into the bowl. Cover with cling film and store in the fridge overnight.

4 When you are ready to bake the bread, remove the dough from the fridge and mould into shape on a piece of Bake-O-Glide or in a tin. Let it rise near the Aga for 45–60 minutes or until it has risen.

Cakes and Baking

5 Bake on the floor of the Roasting Oven for 20–25 minutes or until it sounds hollow when tapped on the underside. (If you are using Bake-O-Glide, put it onto a shallow baking tray and slide the paper off the tray and onto the floor of the oven.) Cool on a wire rack. The great thing about this dough is that you can pull off small amounts to bake and leave the rest in the fridge for up to 2 days.

How can I dry breadcrumbs in the Aga?

To dry breadcrumbs, sprinkle them on a baking tray and 'cook' in the Simmering Oven for 10 minutes then, protecting the lid with a tea towel, place the tray on top and leave there until the breadcrumbs are completely dry. 4-oven Aga owners can use the Warming Oven.

What's the best way to make croûtons?

Cut bread into 2cm cubes. Toss them in olive oil, making sure they are well coated. Spread them on a baking tray and bake on the first set of runners in the Roasting Oven for 8–10 minutes. Keep an eye on them as they burn very easily. Cool on a plate lined with kitchen towel.

How do I thaw frozen bread in the Aga?

Place on the third set of runners in the Roasting Oven for 10–15 minutes, covered with foil if the loaf browns too much while thawing.

What's the best Aga method for cooking pizza?

Line a large inverted baking tray with Bake-O-Glide. Put on the shaped pizza dough and leave the tin next to the Aga for its second rising. Place the tin on the edge of the floor of the Roasting Oven and pull the Bake-O-Glide towards the back of the oven and the tray away, so you are left with dough on the Bake-O-Glide on the oven floor.

Frozen pizza can be cooked directly on the Roasting Oven floor.

Cooking for Crowds

I often have friends to stay for the weekend, but find it hard cooking a full breakfast for everyone. Any advice?

A proper breakfast can be one of the hardest meals to get absolutely right – everything must be cooked to order, usually for large numbers of people.

1 Depending on how many you are cooking for, use either the half-size roasting tin or the full-size one. Line it with Bake-O-Glide, and put mushrooms and tomato halves, cut side up, on the bottom of the tin. Drizzle over a little oil and seasoning. Place the grill rack on top and put the sausages on the rack over the mushrooms and tomatoes (do not prick the sausages).

2 Slide the tin onto the first set of runners in the Roasting Oven, and cook for 10 minutes. Then take the tin out of the oven, turn the sausages and lay the bacon rashers on the grill rack. Put it back into the Roasting Oven for a further 10 minutes. Depending on the thickness of the bacon and the size of the sausages, you may need to adjust the timings.

3 When everything is cooked, put the bacon, sausages, tomatoes and mushrooms onto a warmed platter, cover with foil and transfer to the Simmering Oven to keep warm while you cook the eggs (see page 114–115 for various options). If you want well-done bacon, after you remove the sausages, tomatoes and mushrooms to the platter, take off the grill rack and put the bacon on the bottom of the tin. Place the tin on the floor of the Roasting Oven and let the bacon cook to your liking.

4 To make fried bread, do it in the same way as for well-done bacon, adding a little more oil to the tin if necessary. It will take about 5 minutes for each side.

How do I fry eggs using the Aga?

There are two ways of cooking fried eggs – either in the Aga or on the Aga.

In the Aga: When you remove the sausages, bacon and so on from the tin, add a little more oil to the tin and put it on the Roasting Oven floor to get really hot. When the oil is hot, crack the eggs into the tin one at a time. The large tin will hold 6 large eggs and the half-size tin 3 large eggs. Baste the eggs with the fat and put the tin back into the oven for 3 minutes or until they are cooked to your liking.

On the Aga: Open the Simmering Plate lid and either grease it with a little oil, or use a round pre-cut circle of Bake-O-Glide and put it directly onto the Simmering Plate surface. Drizzle a little oil onto a piece of kitchen paper and rub it over the plate. Crack the egg onto the hot surface and close the lid. The egg will cook in about 2 minutes. The Simmering Plate surface can hold about 3 large eggs at a time. (If your Aga has a dented lid, check to see whether it touches the top of the egg when closed. If it does, leave the lid open. The egg will take a little longer to cook.)

What's the Aga method for scrambling eggs?

Cook scrambled eggs in melted butter in a non-stick saucepan on the Simmering Plate.

What's the best way to poach eggs?

Fill a saucepan with water and place on the Simmering Plate. When it has reached a gentle simmer, swirl the water with a spoon to form a whirlpool. Crack the egg into the water and poach for about 2 minutes. Eggs must be really fresh.

How do I make Aga toast?

Put a slice of bread in the Aga toasting rack and place it on the Boiling Plate Close the lid but keep an eye on it as it will toast very quickly; turn over to do the other side.

To stop very fresh bread from sticking to the toaster, heat the rack first on the Boiling Plate before inserting the bread. If you like crispy toast, leave the Boiling Plate lid open.

What are your hints and tips for cooking Christmas lunch?

Many new Aga owners worry about running out of heat when cooking this huge meal, so it's important to plan your timetable. This timetable is based on a 7kg turkey, to be served at 2pm. Cook stuffing in a dish, rather than inside the bird, so that it can be made in advance and reheated.

7:30am

Remove the turkey from the refrigerator, place a halved onion inside and season the cavity.

8:15am

Put the turkey in the oven (see page 59 for instructions) and baste with melted butter every 30 minutes. If using the Warming Oven in a 4-oven Aga, put in the plates and serving dishes.

11:30am

Prepare bacon rolls and chipolatas. Re-heat bread sauce (made the day before) and place it in a jug with butter on top to melt over the surface, keep warm.

12:00pm

Start steaming the Christmas pudding. Bring to the boil on the Boiling Plate, then transfer to the Simmering Oven for 3 hours.

12:45pm

If you are cooking vegetables conventionally, roast the potatoes and prepare saucepans of boiling water for any other vegetables. Re-heat the stuffing.

1:15pm

Remove the turkey from the oven, cover loosely with foil and let it rest. Make the gravy (see page 66) and keep warm.

1:30pm

Check chipolatas and bacon rolls, remove and keep warm. Put in 'get ahead' roast potatoes (see page 81).

1:45pm

Put Brussels sprouts on to cook or put in 'get ahead' blanched vegetables (see page 80). While they are cooking, transfer the other food into serving dishes and carve the turkey. Check Christmas pudding.

2:00pm

Serve Christmas lunch.

I frequently cook Sunday lunch for friends and family. What's your advice on planning the cooking?

When cooking a traditional Sunday lunch with all the trimmings, it's essential to plan ahead – see my tips on page 29. Pages 53–61 provide information and cooking times for different joints of meat. Also, try cooking vegetables using the Aga get-ahead methods (see page 79–81).

How do I cook Yorkshire pudding in the Aga?

Prepare and cook the Yorkshire pudding earlier in the morning and set aside, then simply re-heat for 8 minutes in the Roasting Oven.

Cooking for Crowds

Everyday Food

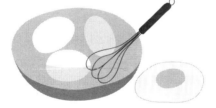

How do I cook pasta using the Aga?

Pasta can be cooked very easily on the Boiling or Simmering Plate. Bring a large pot of water to the boil, generously add salt, then when the water reaches a rolling boil, add the pasta and cook for however many minutes the packet instructions say.

What's the best way to cook rice on the Aga?

This is such an easy way to cook rice and once you try it you won't want to cook rice any other way! It is entirely up to you whether you rinse the rice. As a general rule, use just under double the amount of liquid to rice.

Put the rice, water and the salt into a large saucepan and bring it up to the boil on the Boiling Plate. Stir it once, then cover with a lid and put it on the floor of the Simmering Oven for 18–20 minutes (brown rice will take 30–40 minutes). Remove it from the oven and take the lid off. Fluff up the rice with a fork and cover the pan with a clean tea towel to absorb some of the steam, and then serve.

Everyday Food

Toasted sandwiches are a favourite snack, but how do I cook them on the Aga?

These are so easy and are great for ravenous teenagers! Butter two slices of bread. Place your filling (such as ham and grated cheese) on one unbuttered side and top with the other slice, again buttered side facing outwards, and press together. Place a piece of Bake-O-Glide on the Simmering Plate and lift the sandwich onto it. Close the lid and cook for 2–3 minutes. Open the lid, flip the sandwich over, close the lid and cooker for a further 2–3 minutes or until the bread is golden.

I've heard you can cook porridge overnight in the Aga – how do you do this?

For each serving, place 75g pinhead oatmeal and 600ml water in a pan and bring to the boil on the Boiling Plate, then transfer to the Simmering Plate for 2 minutes. Meanwhile, put the grid shelf on the Simmering Oven floor. Cover the pan with a lid and place on the grid shelf. Leave overnight. Stir well before serving and add brown sugar and cream.

As overnight can mean anything from 6 to 12 hours, another way to cook the porridge is to follow these instructions but put it at the back of the Aga on the hot black enamel surface instead of inside the Simmering Oven.

How do I melt chocolate or butter on the Aga?

Break up the chocolate into pieces, put it into a bowl and stand it on the black top of the Aga, to the left of the Boiling Plate and it will melt in no time at all.

I like to roast my own coffee beans, but how do I use the Aga for this?

To roast green coffee beans, spread the beans out in the large roasting tin. Hang the tin on the first set of runners in the Roasting Oven for 25–30 minutes or until the oils start to run and the beans turn golden brown. Shake the pan three or four times during cooking to roast evenly.

How do I heat convenience food in the Aga?

Simply place the foil packet on a baking tray and slide it onto the third or fourth set of runners in the Roasting Oven and dinner is ready in no time at all. Because the Aga is on 24 hours a day, there is no waiting for ovens to heat up. So take out a store-bought lasagne and garlic bread from the freezer and it will cook in a jiffy.

Useful
Addresses

Amy Willcock
www.amywillcock.co.uk

Chic Kit (Amy's range of textiles)
ICTC
Tel: 01603 488019
www.ictc.co.uk

Aga-Rayburn
Tel: 01952 642000
www.aga-rayburn.co.uk

Bake-O-Glide
Tel: 01706 224790
www.bake-o-glide.co.uk

INDEX

Index

Index